Lily was about to start her very first day at Bright Star Preschool. As she stood outside the school with her mom, her heart pounded with a mix of excitement and nervousness. "What if I can't make any friends?" she wondered aloud.

Her mom knelt down to her level and gave her a reassuring hug.

"Just be yourself, sweetheart. Remember to smile, say hello, and be kind. If you see someone who looks lonely, invite them to play. You'll make friends before you know it!"

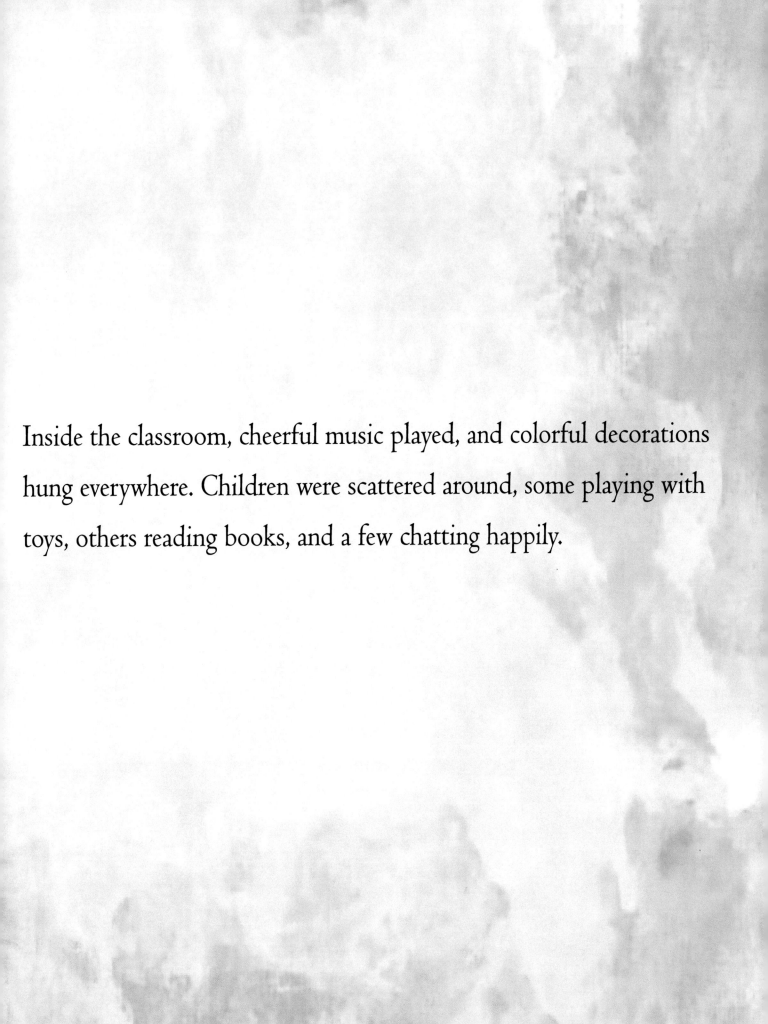

Inside the classroom, cheerful music played, and colorful decorations hung everywhere. Children were scattered around, some playing with toys, others reading books, and a few chatting happily.

Lily took a deep breath and decided to try her mom's advice. She spotted a girl stacking blocks by herself. Gathering her courage, she walked over with a friendly smile. "Hi, I'm Lily. Can I help you build?"

The girl looked up and smiled back. "Sure! I'm Mia. I'm making a tower."

"Maybe we can make it even taller together," Lily suggested.

"Great idea!" Mia agreed.

As they built the tower, Lily made sure to:

- **Share Ideas:** She asked, "What if we add a bridge here?" This made Mia feel included and valued.
- **Listen Actively:** When Mia talked about her favorite colors, Lily listened and asked questions. "You like purple too? What's your favorite thing that's purple?"

After the tower reached the sky (or so it seemed), another child wandered over. "Wow, that's cool!" he said.

"Thanks!" Lily replied. "I'm Lily, and this is Mia. Do you want to build with us?"

"Yes, please! I'm Noah," he said, joining them.

During art time, Lily noticed a boy sitting alone, drawing quietly. Remembering her mom's advice to include others, she walked over. "Hi, your drawing is really good! We're making a big mural with everyone. Do you want to add yours?"

The boy looked up, surprised but pleased. "Okay! I'm Ethan."

"Awesome! I'm Lily. Come on, let's put it up together," she said.

At snack time, Lily practiced sharing. She had some extra apple slices.
"Would anyone like to try an apple slice?" she offered.

"Yes, please!" said a girl with braids. "I'm Ava."

"Nice to meet you, Ava!" Lily said, handing her an apple slice.

Later, on the playground, Lily saw a group of kids playing tag. She noticed a girl standing off to the side, watching. Lily remembered to be inclusive. She ran over and asked, "Hi, do you want to play tag with us? It's lots of fun!"

The girl's face lit up. "I'd love to! I'm Sophia."

"Great! Let's go!" Lily took her hand, and they joined the game together.

Throughout the day, Lily also:

- **Gave Compliments:** "I like your dinosaur shirt!" she told a boy named Max. This made Max smile and start a conversation about dinosaurs.

- **Helped Others:** When Emma dropped her crayons, Lily helped pick them up. "Thank you," Emma said gratefully.

- **Asked to Join In:** When she saw a group playing a game she didn't know, she asked, "Can you show me how to play?" They were happy to teach her.

- **Used Kind Words:** She made sure to say "please," "thank you," and "you're welcome," which made others feel respected.

As the day drew to a close, Miss Harper gathered everyone in a circle. "Let's share one fun thing we did today," she said.

When it was Lily's turn, she said, "I made lots of new friends by sharing and asking people to play!"

Miss Harper smiled. "That's wonderful, Lily. Making friends is all about being kind and open to others."

When Lily's mom arrived to pick her up, Lily ran to her excitedly. "Mom, I made so many friends today!"

"That's fantastic! How did you do it?" her mom asked.

"I smiled, said hello, shared my toys, and invited others to join in," Lily explained proudly.

Her mom hugged her tight. "I'm so proud of you for being such a good friend."

That evening, as Lily got ready for bed, she thought about all the new friends she had made. She realized that making friends wasn't so scary after all. It just took a smile, kindness, and the courage to reach out.

"I can't wait for tomorrow," she whispered to her favorite stuffed animal. "There are so many more friends to make and fun things to do!"

About the Author

Claire Hartwell has a passion for reading and for writing inspirational children's books which explore themes of kindness, friendship, persistence, embracing challenges, inclusivity, empathy, courage and resilience, using her story characters to model such intent and behaviours. She firmly believes in fostering a growth mindset in children and modelling early social skills.

She lives with her three teenage daughters, husband, dog and cat and enjoys precious time with her family and friends when she is not working on writing inspirational, engaging and educational adventures for young children.

"Thank you for purchasing and reading my book. I am extremely grateful and hope you found value in reading it with your children. Please consider sharing it with friends or family and leaving a review online. Your feedback and support are always appreciated".

Warmly, Claire

Made in United States
North Haven, CT
07 January 2025

64136473R00015